LOVE POETRY THROUGH THE AGES:
AN ANTHOLOGY

Dog's Tail Books

ISBN: 978-1530477487

© Will Jonson & Dog's Tail Books

Find us at www.dogstailbooks.co.uk

CONTENTS

Sir Thomas Wyatt

They Flee From Me	9
And Wilt thou Leave me Thus?	10
Whoso List to Hunt, I Know where is an Hind	11
I Find no Peace	12

Henry Howard, Earl of Surrey

"Alas, so all things now do hold their peace!"	13
Complaint of the Absence of Her Love Being Upon the Sea	14

Sir Philip Sidney

Astrophil and Stella 1: Loving in truth, and fain in verse my love to show	16
Astrophil and Stella 41: Having this day my horse, my hand, my lance	17
Astrophil and Stella 90: Stella, think not that I by verse seek fame	18
Astrophil and Stella 107: Stella, since thou so right a princess art	19

Christopher Marlowe

The Passionate Shepherd to His Love	20

Sir Walter Raleigh

The Nymph's Reply to the Shepherd	21

William Shakespeare

Sonnet 18	23
Sonnet 19	23
Sonnet 40	24
Sonnet 57	24
Sonnet 61	25
Sonnet 71	25

Sonnet 91	26
Sonnet 116	26
Sonnet 129	27
Sonnet 130	27

Michael Drayton

Idea 20: An evil spirit, your beauty, haunts me still	28
Idea 43: Why should your fair eyes with such sovereign grace	29
Idea 61: Since there's no help, come let us kiss and part	30

John Donne

The Good Morrow	31
The Flea	32
The Sun Rising	33
Song: Go Catch a Falling Star	34
Song: Sweetest Love, I do not go	35
On His Mistress Going to Bed	37

Ben Jonson

Song to Celia: Drink to me only with thine eyes	39
Song to Celia: Come, my Celia, let us prove	40

Robert Herrick

Delight in Disorder	41
The Night Piece, to Julia	42
To Anthea	43
To Anthea, who may command him anything	44
Upon Julia's Clothes	45

Andrew Marvell

The Unfortunate Lover	46
To His Coy Mistress	49
The Picture of Little T. C. in a Prospect of Flowers	51
The Gallery	53
Young Love	56
The Definition of Love	58
The Fair Singer	60
Damon the Mower	61
The Mower's Song	65
The Mower to the Glow Worms	67

Richard Lovelace

Song to Amarantha, that she would Dishevel her hair	68
To Althea, from Prison	70
The Scrutinie	72
To Lucasta, Going to the Wars	73

Sir John Suckling

Song: Out upon it, I have loved	74
Song: Why so pale and wan fond lover?	75

John Wilmot, Earl of Rochester

A Song of a Young Lady to her Ancient Lover	76
Absent from Thee I languish still	77
To His Mistress	78

Aphra Behn

Oh, How the Hand the Lover Ought to Prize	80
Love Armed	81

Love's Witness	82
The Willing Mistress	83

William Blake

Never Seek to Tell Thy Love	84
The Sick Rose	84
The Clod and the Pebble	85
The Garden of Love	86

Robert Burns

A Red, Red Rose	87
Ae Fond Kiss	88

William Wordsworth

She Dwelt among the Untrodden Ways	89
She was a Phantom of Delight	90
Why are thou silent! Is thy love a plant?	92

Lord Byron

She Walks in Beauty	93
When we two parted	94

Percy Bysshe Shelley

To Jane: The Invitation	95
The Indian Serenade	98
Love's Philosophy	99

John Keats

Bright star, would I were as steadfast as though art	100
This living hand, now warm and capable	100

Fanny	101
La Belle Dame Sans Merci: A Ballad	102

Emily Brontë
Remembrance	105
Love and Friendship	107

Elizabeth Barrett Browning
If thou must love me let it be for nought	108
My letters! All dead paper ... mute and white	109
First time he kissed me, but only kissed	110
How do I love thee? Let me count the ways	111
Beloved, thou hast brought me many flowers	112

Christina Rossetti
I loved you first, but afterwards your love	113
I wish I could remember that first day	114
Remember	115
When I am dead, my dearest	116
Echo	117

Thomas Hardy
Neutral Tones	118
The Voice	119
The Phantom Horsewoman	120
The Ruined Maid	122

Ernest Dowson
Non sum qualis eram bonae sub regno Cynarae	124
What is love?	125

Charlotte Mew

The Farmer's Bride   126

SIR THOMAS WYATT

They Flee From Me

They flee from me that sometime did me seek
With naked foot, stalking in my chamber.
I have seen them gentle, tame, and meek,
That now are wild and do not remember
That sometime they put themself in danger
To take bread at my hand; and now they range,
Busily seeking with a continual change.

Thanked be fortune it hath been otherwise
Twenty times better; but once in special,
In thin array after a pleasant guise,
When her loose gown from her shoulders did fall,
And she me caught in her arms long and small;
Therewithall sweetly did me kiss
And softly said, "Dear heart, how like you this?"

It was no dream: I lay broad waking.
But all is turned thorough my gentleness
Into a strange fashion of forsaking;
And I have leave to go of her goodness,
And she also, to use newfangleness.
But since that I so kindly am served
I would fain know what she hath deserved.

And Wilt thou Leave me Thus?

And wilt thou leave me thus?
Say nay, say nay, for shame,
To save thee from the blame
Of all my grief and grame;
And wilt thou leave me thus?
Say nay, say nay!

And wilt thou leave me thus,
That hath loved thee so long
In wealth and woe among?
And is thy heart so strong
As for to leave me thus?
Say nay, say nay!

And wilt thou leave me thus,
That hath given thee my heart
Never for to depart,
Nother for pain nor smart;
And wilt thou leave me thus?
Say nay, say nay!

And wilt thou leave me thus
And have no more pity
Of him that loveth thee?
Hélas, thy cruelty!
And wilt thou leave me thus?
Say nay, say nay!

Whoso List to Hunt, I Know where is an Hind

Whoso list to hunt, I know where is an hind,
But as for me, *hélas*, I may no more.
The vain travail hath wearied me so sore,
I am of them that farthest cometh behind.
Yet may I by no means my wearied mind
Draw from the deer, but as she fleeth afore
Fainting I follow. I leave off therefore,
Sithens in a net I seek to hold the wind.
Who list her hunt, I put him out of doubt,
As well as I may spend his time in vain.
And graven with diamonds in letters plain
There is written, her fair neck round about:
Noli me tangere, for Caesar's I am,
And wild for to hold, though I seem tame.

I Find no Peace

I find no peace, and all my war is done.
I fear and hope. I burn and freeze like ice.
I fly above the wind, yet can I not arise;
And nought I have, and all the world I season.
That loseth nor locketh holdeth me in prison
And holdeth me not—yet can I scape no wise—
Nor letteth me live nor die at my device,
And yet of death it giveth me occasion.
Without eyen I see, and without tongue I plain.
I desire to perish, and yet I ask health.
I love another, and thus I hate myself.
I feed me in sorrow and laugh in all my pain;
Likewise displeaseth me both life and death,
And my delight is causer of this strife.

HENRY HOWARD, EARL OF SURREY

"Alas, so all things now do hold their peace!"

Alas, so all things now do hold their peace!
   Heaven and earth disturbèd in no thing;
The beasts, the air, the birds their song do cease,
   The nightès car the stars about doth bring;
Calm is the sea; the waves work less and less:
   So am not I, whom love, alas! doth wring,
Bringing before my face the great increase
   Of my desires, whereat I weep and sing,
In joy and woe, as in a doubtful case.
   For my sweet thoughts sometime do pleasure bring:
But by and by, the cause of my disease
   Gives me a pang that inwardly doth sting,
When that I think what grief it is again
To live and lack the thing should rid my pain.

Complaint of the Absence of Her Love Being Upon the Sea

O happy dames, that may embrace
   The fruit of your delight,
Help to bewail the woeful case
   And eke the heavy plight
Of me, that wonted to rejoice
The fortune of my pleasant choice;
Good ladies, help to fill my mourning voice.

In ship, freight with remembrance
   Of thoughts and pleasures past,
He sails that hath in governance
   My life while it will last;
With scalding sighs, for lack of gale,
Furthering his hope, that is his sail,
Toward me, the sweet port of his avail.

Alas! how oft in dreams I see
   Those eyes that were my food;
Which sometime so delighted me,
   That yet they do me good;
Wherewith I wake with his return,
Whose absent flame did make me burn:
But when I find the lack, Lord, how I mourn!

When other lovers in arms across
   Rejoice their chief delight.
Drowned in tears, to mourn my loss
   I stand the bitter night

In my window, where I may see
Before the winds how the clouds flee.
Lo! what a mariner love hath made of me!

And in green waves when the salt flood
   Doth rise by rage of wind,
A thousand fancies in that mood
   Assail my restless mind.
Alas! now drencheth my sweet foe,
That with the spoil of my heart did go,
And left me; but, alas! why did he so?

And when the seas wax calm again
   To chase fro me annoy,
My doubtful hope doth cause me pain;
   So dread cuts off my joy.
Thus is my wealth mingled with woe,
And of each thought a doubt doth grow;
"Now he comes! Will he come? Alas, no, no!"

SIR PHILIP SIDNEY

Astrophil and Stella 1: Loving in truth, and fain in verse my love to show

Loving in truth, and fain in verse my love to show,
That she, dear she, might take some pleasure of my pain,—
Pleasure might cause her read, reading might make her know,
Knowledge might pity win, and pity grace obtain,—
I sought fit words to paint the blackest face of woe;
Studying inventions fine her wits to entertain,
Oft turning others' leaves, to see if thence would flow
Some fresh and fruitful showers upon my sunburn'd brain.
But words came halting forth, wanting invention's stay;
Invention, Nature's child, fled step-dame Study's blows;
And others' feet still seem'd but strangers in my way.
Thus great with child to speak and helpless in my throes,
Biting my truant pen, beating myself for spite,
"Fool," said my Muse to me, "look in thy heart, and write."

Astrophil and Stella 41: Having this day my horse, my hand, my lance

Having this day my horse, my hand, my lance
Guided so well that I obtain'd the prize,
Both by the judgment of the English eyes
And of some sent from that sweet enemy France;
Horsemen my skill in horsemanship advance,
Town folks my strength; a daintier judge applies
His praise to sleight which from good use doth rise;
Some lucky wits impute it but to chance;
Others, because of both sides I do take
My blood from them who did excel in this,
Think Nature me a man of arms did make.
How far they shot awry! The true cause is,
Stella look'd on, and from her heav'nly face
Sent forth the beams which made so fair my race.

Astrophil and Stella 90: Stella, think not that I by verse seek fame

Stella, think not that I by verse seek fame,

Who seek, who hope, who love, who live but thee;

Thine eyes my pride, thy lips my history;

If thou praise not, all other praise is shame.

Nor so ambitious am I, as to frame

A nest for my young praise in laurel tree:

In truth I sweare, I wish not there should be

Graved in mine epitaph a Poet's name:

Nay if I would, could I just title make,

That any laud to me thereof should grow,

Without my plumes from others' wings I take.

For nothing from my wit or will doth flow,

Since all my words thy beauty doth endite,

And love doth hold my hand, and makes me write.

Astrophil and Stella 107: Stella, since thou so right a princess art

Stella, since thou so right a princess art
Of all the powers which life bestows on me,
There ere by them aught undertaken be
They first resort unto that sovereign part;
Sweet, for a while give respite to my heart,
Which pants as though it still should leap to thee,
And on my thoughts give thy lieutenancy
To this great cause, which needs both use and art,
And as a queen, who from her presence sends
Whom she employs, dismiss from thee my wit,
Till it have wrought what thy own will attends.
On servants' shame oft master's blame doth sit.
Oh let not fools in me thy works reprove,
And scorning say, "See what it is to love."

The Passionate Shepherd to His Love
BY CHRISTOPHER MARLOWE

Come live with me and be my love,
And we will all the pleasures prove,
That Valleys, groves, hills, and fields,
Woods, or steepy mountain yields.

And we will sit upon the Rocks,
Seeing the Shepherds feed their flocks,
By shallow Rivers to whose falls
Melodious birds sing Madrigals.

And I will make thee beds of Roses
And a thousand fragrant posies,
A cap of flowers, and a kirtle
Embroidered all with leaves of Myrtle;

A gown made of the finest wool
Which from our pretty Lambs we pull;
Fair lined slippers for the cold,
With buckles of the purest gold;

A belt of straw and Ivy buds,
With Coral clasps and Amber studs:
And if these pleasures may thee move,
Come live with me, and be my love.

The Shepherds' Swains shall dance and sing
For thy delight each May-morning:
If these delights thy mind may move,

Then live with me, and be my love.

The Nymph's Reply to the Shepherd
BY SIR WALTER RALEGH

If all the world and love were young,
And truth in every Shepherd's tongue,
These pretty pleasures might me move,
To live with thee, and be thy love.

Time drives the flocks from field to fold,
When Rivers rage and Rocks grow cold,
And *Philomel* becometh dumb,
The rest complains of cares to come.

The flowers do fade, and wanton fields,
To wayward winter reckoning yields,
A honey tongue, a heart of gall,
Is fancy's spring, but sorrow's fall.

Thy gowns, thy shoes, thy beds of Roses,
Thy cap, thy kirtle, and thy posies
Soon break, soon wither, soon forgotten:
In folly ripe, in reason rotten.

Thy belt of straw and Ivy buds,
The Coral clasps and amber studs,
All these in me no means can move
To come to thee and be thy love.

But could youth last, and love still breed,
Had joys no date, nor age no need,
Then these delights my mind might move
To live with thee, and be thy love.

WILLIAM SHAKESPEARE

SONNET 18

Shall I compare thee to a summer's day?
Thou art more lovely and more temperate:
Rough winds do shake the darling buds of May,
And summer's lease hath all too short a date:
Sometime too hot the eye of heaven shines,
And often is his gold complexion dimm'd;
And every fair from fair sometime declines,
By chance, or nature's changing course, untrimm'd;
But thy eternal summer shall not fade
Nor lose possession of that fair thou ow'st;
Nor shall Death brag thou wander'st in his shade,
When in eternal lines to time thou grow'st;
So long as men can breathe or eyes can see,
So long lives this, and this gives life to thee.

SONNET 19

Devouring Time, blunt thou the lion's paws,
And make the earth devour her own sweet brood;
Pluck the keen teeth from the fierce tiger's jaws,
And burn the long-lived phoenix in her blood;
Make glad and sorry seasons as thou fleet'st,
And do whate'er thou wilt, swift-footed Time,
To the wide world and all her fading sweets;
But I forbid thee one most heinous crime:
O, carve not with thy hours my love's fair brow,
Nor draw no lines there with thine antique pen;
Him in thy course untainted do allow
For beauty's pattern to succeeding men.
Yet, do thy worst, old Time: despite thy wrong,
My love shall in my verse ever live young.

SONNET 40

Take all my loves, my love, yea, take them all;
What hast thou then more than thou hadst before?
No love, my love, that thou may'st true love call;
All mine was thine before thou hadst this more.
Then if for my love thou my love receivest,
I cannot blame thee for my love thou usest;
But yet be blamed, if thou thyself deceivest
By wilful taste of what thyself refusest.
I do forgive thy robbery, gentle thief,
Although thou steal thee all my poverty;
And yet, love knows, it is a greater grief
To bear love's wrong than hate's known injury.
   Lascivious grace, in whom all ill well shows,
   Kill me with spites; yet we must not be foes.

SONNET 57

Being your slave, what should I do but tend
Upon the hours and times of your desire?
I have no precious time at all to spend,
Nor services to do, till you require.
Nor dare I chide the world-without-end hour
Whilst I, my sovereign, watch the clock for you,
Nor think the bitterness of absence sour
When you have bid your servant once adieu;
Nor dare I question with my jealous thought
Where you may be, or your affairs suppose,
But, like a sad slave, stay and think of nought
Save, where you are how happy you make those.
   So true a fool is love that in your will,
   Though you do any thing, he thinks no ill.

SONNET 61

Is it thy will thy image should keep open
My heavy eyelids to the weary night?
Dost thou desire my slumbers should be broken,
While shadows, like to thee, do mock my sight?
Is it thy spirit that thou send'st from thee
So far from home into my deeds to pry,
To find out shames and idle hours in me,
The scope and tenor of thy jealousy?
O, no! thy love, though much, is not so great:
It is my love that keeps mine eye awake;
Mine own true love that doth my rest defeat,
To play the watchman ever for thy sake:
   For thee watch I whilst thou dost wake elsewhere,
   From me far off, with others all too near.

SONNET 71

No longer mourn for me when I am dead
Then you shall hear the surly sullen bell
Give warning to the world that I am fled
From this vile world, with vilest worms to dwell:
Nay, if you read this line, remember not
The hand that writ it; for I love you so
That I in your sweet thoughts would be forgot
If thinking on me then should make you woe.
O, if, I say, you look upon this verse
When I perhaps compounded am with clay,
Do not so much as my poor name rehearse.
But let your love even with my life decay,
   Lest the wise world should look into your moan
   And mock you with me after I am gone.

SONNET 91

Some glory in their birth, some in their skill,
Some in their wealth, some in their body's force,
Some in their garments, though new-fangled ill;
Some in their hawks and hounds, some in their horse;
And every humour hath his adjunct pleasure,
Wherein it finds a joy above the rest:
But these particulars are not my measure;
All these I better in one general best.
Thy love is better than high birth to me,
Richer than wealth, prouder than garments' cost,
Of more delight than hawks or horses be;
And having thee, of all men's pride I boast:
   Wretched in this alone, that thou may'st take
   All this away, and me most wretched make.

SONNET 116

Let me not to the marriage of true minds
Admit impediments. Love is not love
Which alters when it alteration finds,
Or bends with the remover to remove:
O no; it is an ever-fixed mark,
That looks on tempests, and is never shaken;
It is the star to every wandering bark,
Whose worth's unknown, although his height be taken.
Love's not Time's fool, though rosy lips and cheeks
Within his bending sickle's compass come;
Love alters not with his brief hours and weeks,
But bears it out even to the edge of doom.
   If this be error and upon me proved,
   I never writ, nor no man ever loved.

SONNET 129

The expense of spirit in a waste of shame
Is lust in action; and till action, lust
Is perjured, murderous, bloody, full of blame,
Savage, extreme, rude, cruel, not to trust,
Enjoy'd no sooner but despised straight,
Past reason hunted, and no sooner had
Past reason hated, as a swallow'd bait
On purpose laid to make the taker mad;
Mad in pursuit and in possession so;
Had, having, and in quest to have, extreme;
A bliss in proof, and proved, a very woe;
Before, a joy proposed; behind, a dream.
   All this the world well knows; yet none knows well
   To shun the heaven that leads men to this hell.

SONNET 130

My mistress' eyes are nothing like the sun;
Coral is far more red than her lips' red;
If snow be white, why then her breasts are dun;
If hairs be wires, black wires grow on her head.
I have seen roses damask'd, red and white,
But no such roses see I in her cheeks;
And in some perfumes is there more delight
Than in the breath that from my mistress reeks.
I love to hear her speak, yet well I know
That music hath a far more pleasing sound;
I grant I never saw a goddess go;
My mistress, when she walks, treads on the ground:
   And yet, by heaven, I think my love as rare
   As any she belied with false compare.

MICHAEL DRAYTON

Idea 20: An evil spirit, your beauty, haunts me still

An evil spirit, your beauty, haunts me still,
Wherewith, alas, I have been long possess'd,
Which ceaseth not to tempt me to each ill,
Nor gives me once but one poor minute's rest.
In me it speaks, whether I sleep or wake;
And when by means to drive it out I try,
With greater torments then it me doth take,
And tortures me in most extremity.
Before my face it lays down my despairs,
And hastes me on unto a sudden death;
Now tempting me to drown myself in tears,
And then in sighing to give up my breath.
Thus am I still provok'd to every evil
By this good-wicked spirit, sweet angel-devil.

Idea 43: Why should your fair eyes with such sovereign grace

Why should your fair eyes with such sovereign grace

Disperse their rays on every vulgar spirit,

Whilst I in darkness in the self-same place

Get not one glance to recompense my merit?

So doth the ploughman gaze the wandering star,

And only rest contented with the light,

That never learned what constellations are,

Beyond the bent of his unknowing sight,

O! why should beauty, custom to obey,

To their gross sense apply herself so ill?

Would God I were as ignorant as they,

When I am made unhappy by my skill;

Only compelled on this poor good to boast,

Heavens are not kind to them that know them most.

Idea 61: Since there's no help, come let us kiss and part

Since there's no help, come let us kiss and part.
Nay, I have done, you get no more of me;
And I am glad, yea glad with all my heart,
That thus so cleanly I myself can free.
Shake hands for ever, cancel all our vows,
And when we meet at any time again,
Be it not seen in either of our brows
That we one jot of former love retain.
Now at the last gasp of Love's latest breath,
When, his pulse failing, Passion speechless lies;
When Faith is kneeling by his bed of death,
And Innocence is closing up his eyes—
Now, if thou wouldst, when all have given him over,
From death to life thou might'st him yet recover!

JOHN DONNE

The Good-Morrow

I wonder, by my troth, what thou and I
Did, till we loved? Were we not weaned till then?
But sucked on country pleasures, childishly?
Or snorted we in the Seven Sleepers' den?
'Twas so; but this, all pleasures fancies be.
If ever any beauty I did see,
Which I desired, and got, 'twas but a dream of thee.

And now good-morrow to our waking souls,
Which watch not one another out of fear;
For love, all love of other sights controls,
And makes one little room an everywhere.
Let sea-discoverers to new worlds have gone,
Let maps to other, worlds on worlds have shown,
Let us possess one world, each hath one, and is one.

My face in thine eye, thine in mine appears,
And true plain hearts do in the faces rest;
Where can we find two better hemispheres,
Without sharp north, without declining west?
Whatever dies, was not mixed equally;
If our two loves be one, or, thou and I
Love so alike, that none do slacken, none can die.

The Flea

Mark but this flea, and mark in this,
How little that which thou deniest me is;
It sucked me first, and now sucks thee,
And in this flea our two bloods mingled be;
Thou know'st that this cannot be said
A sin, nor shame, nor loss of maidenhead,
   Yet this enjoys before it woo,
     And pampered swells with one blood made of two,
     And this, alas, is more than we would do.

Oh stay, three lives in one flea spare,
Where we almost, nay more than married are.
This flea is you and I, and this
Our mariage bed, and marriage temple is;
Though parents grudge, and you, w'are met,
And cloistered in these living walls of jet.
   Though use make you apt to kill me,
     Let not to that, self-murder added be,
     And sacrilege, three sins in killing three.

Cruel and sudden, hast thou since
Purpled thy nail, in blood of innocence?
Wherein could this flea guilty be,
Except in that drop which it sucked from thee?
Yet thou triumph'st, and say'st that thou
Find'st not thy self, nor me the weaker now;
   'Tis true; then learn how false, fears be:
     Just so much honor, when thou yield'st to me,

Will waste, as this flea's death took life from thee.

The Sun Rising

        Busy old fool, unruly sun,
        Why dost thou thus,
Through windows, and through curtains call on us?
Must to thy motions lovers' seasons run?
        Saucy pedantic wretch, go chide
        Late school boys and sour prentices,
      Go tell court huntsmen that the king will ride,
      Call country ants to harvest offices,
Love, all alike, no season knows nor clime,
Nor hours, days, months, which are the rags of time.

        Thy beams, so reverend and strong
        Why shouldst thou think?
I could eclipse and cloud them with a wink,
But that I would not lose her sight so long;
        If her eyes have not blinded thine,
        Look, and tomorrow late, tell me,
        Whether both th' Indias of spice and mine
        Be where thou leftst them, or lie here with me.
Ask for those kings whom thou saw'st yesterday,
And thou shalt hear, All here in one bed lay.

        She's all states, and all princes, I,
        Nothing else is.
Princes do but play us; compared to this,
All honor's mimic, all wealth alchemy.

    Thou, sun, art half as happy as we,
        In that the world's contracted thus.
  Thine age asks ease, and since thy duties be
      To warm the world, that's done in warming us.
Shine here to us, and thou art everywhere;
This bed thy center is, these walls, thy sphere.

Song: Go and catch a falling star

Go and catch a falling star,
    Get with child a mandrake root,
Tell me where all past years are,
    Or who cleft the devil's foot,
Teach me to hear mermaids singing,
Or to keep off envy's stinging,
      And find
      What wind
Serves to advance an honest mind.

If thou be'st born to strange sights,
    Things invisible to see,
Ride ten thousand days and nights,
    Till age snow white hairs on thee,
Thou, when thou return'st, wilt tell me,
All strange wonders that befell thee,
      And swear,
      No where
Lives a woman true, and fair.

If thou find'st one, let me know,
    Such a pilgrimage were sweet;
Yet do not, I would not go,
    Though at next door we might meet;
Though she were true, when you met her,
And last, till you write your letter,
        Yet she
        Will be
False, ere I come, to two, or three.

Song: Sweetest love, I do not go

Sweetest love, I do not go,
    For weariness of thee,
Nor in hope the world can show
    A fitter love for me;
        But since that I
Must die at last, 'tis best
To use myself in jest
    Thus by feign'd deaths to die.

Yesternight the sun went hence,
    And yet is here today;
He hath no desire nor sense,
    Nor half so short a way:
        Then fear not me,
But believe that I shall make
Speedier journeys, since I take
    More wings and spurs than he.

O how feeble is man's power,
    That if good fortune fall,
Cannot add another hour,
    Nor a lost hour recall!
        But come bad chance,
And we join to'it our strength,
And we teach it art and length,
    Itself o'er us to'advance.

When thou sigh'st, thou sigh'st not wind,
    But sigh'st my soul away;
When thou weep'st, unkindly kind,
    My life's blood doth decay.
        It cannot be
That thou lov'st me, as thou say'st,
If in thine my life thou waste,
    That art the best of me.

Let not thy divining heart
    Forethink me any ill;
Destiny may take thy part,
    And may thy fears fulfil;
        But think that we
Are but turn'd aside to sleep;
They who one another keep
    Alive, ne'er parted be.

To His Mistress Going to Bed

Come, Madam, come, all rest my powers defy,
Until I labour, I in labour lie.
The foe oft-times having the foe in sight,
Is tir'd with standing though he never fight.
Off with that girdle, like heaven's Zone glistering,
But a far fairer world encompassing.
Unpin that spangled breastplate which you wear,
That th'eyes of busy fools may be stopped there.
Unlace yourself, for that harmonious chime,
Tells me from you, that now it is bed time.
Off with that happy busk, which I envy,
That still can be, and still can stand so nigh.
Your gown going off, such beauteous state reveals,
As when from flowery meads th'hill's shadow steals.
Off with that wiry Coronet and shew
The hairy Diadem which on you doth grow:
Now off with those shoes, and then safely tread
In this love's hallow'd temple, this soft bed.
In such white robes, heaven's Angels used to be
Received by men; Thou Angel bringst with thee
A heaven like Mahomet's Paradise; and though
Ill spirits walk in white, we easily know,
By this these Angels from an evil sprite,
Those set our hairs, but these our flesh upright.
    Licence my roving hands, and let them go,
Before, behind, between, above, below.
O my America! my new-found-land,
My kingdom, safeliest when with one man mann'd,

My Mine of precious stones, My Empirie,
How blest am I in this discovering thee!
To enter in these bonds, is to be free;
Then where my hand is set, my seal shall be.
    Full nakedness! All joys are due to thee,
As souls unbodied, bodies uncloth'd must be,
To taste whole joys. Gems which you women use
Are like Atlanta's balls, cast in men's views,
That when a fool's eye lighteth on a Gem,
His earthly soul may covet theirs, not them.
Like pictures, or like books' gay coverings made
For lay-men, are all women thus array'd;
Themselves are mystic books, which only we
(Whom their imputed grace will dignify)
Must see reveal'd. Then since that I may know;
As liberally, as to a Midwife, shew
Thy self: cast all, yea, this white linen hence,
There is no penance due to innocence.
    To teach thee, I am naked first; why then
What needst thou have more covering than a man.

BEN JONSON
Song: to Celia ["Drink to me only with thine eyes"]

Drink to me only with thine eyes,
    And I will pledge with mine;
Or leave a kiss but in the cup,
    And I'll not look for wine.
The thirst that from the soul doth rise
    Doth ask a drink divine;
But might I of Jove's nectar sup,
    I would not change for thine.

I sent thee late a rosy wreath,
    Not so much honouring thee
As giving it a hope, that there
    It could not withered be.
But thou thereon didst only breathe,
    And sent'st it back to me;
Since when it grows, and smells, I swear,
    Not of itself, but thee.

Song: to Celia [Come, my Celia, let us prove]

Come, my Celia, let us prove,
While we can, the sports of love;
Time will not be ours forever;
He at length our good will sever.
Spend not then his gifts in vain.
Suns that set may rise again;
But if once we lose this light,
'Tis with us perpetual night.
Why should we defer our joys?
Fame and rumor are but toys.
Cannot we delude the eyes
Of a few poor household spies,
Or his easier ears beguile,
So removèd by our wile?
'Tis no sin love's fruit to steal;
But the sweet thefts to reveal,
To be taken, to be seen,
These have crimes accounted been.

ROBERT HERRICK
Delight in Disorder

A sweet disorder in the dress
Kindles in clothes a wantonness;
A lawn about the shoulders thrown
Into a fine distraction;
An erring lace, which here and there
Enthrals the crimson stomacher;
A cuff neglectful, and thereby
Ribands to flow confusedly;
A winning wave, deserving note,
In the tempestuous petticoat;
A careless shoe-string, in whose tie
I see a wild civility:
Do more bewitch me, than when art
Is too precise in every part.

The Night Piece, to Julia

Her eyes the glow-worm lend thee,
The shooting stars attend thee;
    And the elves also,
    Whose little eyes glow
Like the sparks of fire, befriend thee.

No Will-o'-th'-Wisp mis-light thee,
Nor snake or slow-worm bite thee;
    But on, on thy way,
    Not making a stay,
Since ghost there's none to affright thee.

Let not the dark thee cumber;
What though the moon does slumber?
    The stars of the night
    Will lend thee their light,
Like tapers clear without number.

Then Julia let me woo thee,
Thus, thus to come unto me;
    And when I shall meet
    Thy silv'ry feet,
My soul I'll pour into thee.

To Anthea

Let's call for Hymen if agreed thou art –
Delays in love but crucify the heart.
Love's thorny tapers yet neglected lie;
Speak thou the word, they'll kindle by and by.
The nimble hours woo us on to wed,
And Genius waits to have us both to bed.
Behold, for us the naked Graces stay
With maunds of roses for us to strew the way.
Besides, the most religious prophet stands
Ready to join as well our hearts as hands.
June yet smiles; but if she chance to chide,
Ill luck 'twill bode to th'bridegroom and the bride.
Tell me Anthea, dost thou fondly dread
The loss of that we call a maidenhead?
Come, I'll instruct thee. Know, the vestal fire
Is not by marriage quenched, but flames the higher.

To Anthea, who may Command him Anything

Bid me to live, and I will live
    Thy protestant to be;
Or bid me love, and I will give
    A loving heart to thee.

A heart as soft, a heart as kind,
    A heart as sound and free,
As in the whole world thou canst find,
    That heart I'll give to thee.

Bid that heart stay, and it will stay,
    To honour thy decree;
Or bid it languish quite away,
    And 't shall do so for thee.

Bid me to weep, and I will weep,
    While I have eyes to see;
And having none, yet I will keep
    A heart to weep for thee.

Bid me despair, and I'll despair,
    Under that cypress tree;
Or bid me die, and I will dare
    E'en death, to die for thee.

Thou art my life, my love, my heart,
    The very eyes of me;
And hast command of every part,

To live and die for thee.

Upon Julia's Clothes

Whenas in silks my Julia goes,
Then, then (methinks) how sweetly flows
That liquefaction of her clothes.

Next, when I cast mine eyes, and see
That brave vibration each way free,
O how that glittering taketh me!

ANDREW MARVELL

The Unfortunate Lover

Alas, how pleasant are their days
With whom the infant Love yet plays!
Sorted by pairs, they still are seen
By fountains cool, and shadows green.
But soon these flames do lose their light,
Like meteors of a summer's night:
Nor can they to that region climb,
To make impression upon time.

'Twas in a shipwreck, when the seas
Ruled, and the winds did what they please,
That my poor lover floating lay,
And, ere brought forth, was cast away:
Till at the last the master-wave
Upon the rock his mother drave;
And there she split against the stone,
In a Caesarean sectión.

The sea him lent those bitter tears
Which at his eyes he always wears;
And from the winds the sighs he bore,
Which through his surging breast do roar.
No day he saw but that which breaks
Through frighted clouds in forkèd streaks,
While round the rattling thunder hurled,
As at the funeral of the world.

While Nature to his birth presents
This masque of quarrelling elements,
A numerous fleet of cormorants black,
That sailed insulting o'er the wrack,
Received into their cruel care
Th' unfortunate and abject heir:
Guardians most fit to entertain
The orphan of the hurricane.

They fed him up with hopes and air,
Which soon digested to despair,
And as one cormorant fed him, still
Another on his heart did bill,
Thus while they famish him, and feast,
He both consumèd, and increased:
And languishèd with doubtful breath,
The amphibíum of life and death.

And now, when angry heaven would

Behold a spectacle of blood,
Fortune and he are called to play
At sharp before it all the day:
And tyrant Love his breast does ply
With all his winged artillery,
Whilst he, betwixt the flames and waves,
Like Ajax, the mad tempest braves.

See how he nak'd and fierce does stand,
Cuffing the thunder with one hand,
While with the other he does lock,
And grapple, with the stubborn rock:
From which he with each wave rebounds,
Torn into flames, and ragg'd with wounds,
And all he 'says, a lover dressed
In his own blood does relish best.

This is the only banneret
That ever Love created yet:
Who though, by the malignant stars,
Forcèd to live in storms and wars,
Yet dying leaves a perfume here,
And music within every ear:
And he in story only rules,
In a field sable a lover gules.

To His Coy Mistress

Had we but world enough and time,
This coyness, lady, were no crime.
We would sit down, and think which way
To walk, and pass our long love's day.
Thou by the Indian Ganges' side
Shouldst rubies find; I by the tide
Of Humber would complain. I would
Love you ten years before the flood,
And you should, if you please, refuse
Till the conversion of the Jews.
My vegetable love should grow
Vaster than empires and more slow;
An hundred years should go to praise
Thine eyes, and on thy forehead gaze;
Two hundred to adore each breast,
But thirty thousand to the rest;
An age at least to every part,
And the last age should show your heart.
For, lady, you deserve this state,
Nor would I love at lower rate.

    But at my back I always hear
Time's wingèd chariot hurrying near;
And yonder all before us lie
Deserts of vast eternity.
Thy beauty shall no more be found;
Nor, in thy marble vault, shall sound
My echoing song; then worms shall try
That long-preserved virginity,

And your quaint honour turn to dust,
And into ashes all my lust;
The grave's a fine and private place,
But none, I think, do there embrace.
    Now therefore, while the youthful hue
Sits on thy skin like morning dew,
And while thy willing soul transpires
At every pore with instant fires,
Now let us sport us while we may,
And now, like amorous birds of prey,
Rather at once our time devour
Than languish in his slow-chapped power.
Let us roll all our strength and all
Our sweetness up into one ball,
And tear our pleasures with rough strife
Through the iron gates of life:
Thus, though we cannot make our sun
Stand still, yet we will make him run.

The Picture of Little T. C. in a Prospect of Flowers

See with what simplicity
This nymph begins her golden days!
In the green grass she loves to lie,
And there with her fair aspect tames
The wilder flowers, and gives them names:
But only with the roses plays;
           And them does tell
What colour best becomes them, and what smell.

Who can foretell for what high cause
This Darling of the Gods was born!
Yet this is she whose chaster laws
The wanton Love shall one day fear,
And, under her command severe,
See his bow broke and ensigns torn.
           Happy, who can
Appease this virtuous enemy of man!

O, then let me in time compound,
And parley with those conquering eyes;
Ere they have tried their force to wound,
Ere, with their glancing wheels, they drive
In triumph over hearts that strive,
And them that yield but more despise.
           Let me be laid,
Where I may see thy glories from some shade.

Meantime, whilst every verdant thing

Itself does at thy beauty charm,
Reform the errors of the spring;
Make that the tulips may have share
Of sweetness, seeing they are fair;
And roses of their thorns disarm:
                    But most procure
That violets may a longer age endure.

But, O young beauty of the woods,
Whom Nature courts with fruits and flowers,
Gather the flowers, but spare the buds;
Lest Flora angry at thy crime,
To kill her infants in their prime,
Do quickly make the example yours;
                    And, ere we see,
Nip in the blossom all our hopes and thee.

The Gallery

Clora, come view my soul, and tell
Whether I have contrived it well.
Now all its several lodgings lie
Composed into one gallery;
And the great arras-hangings, made
Of various faces, by are laid;
That, for all furniture, you'll find
Only your picture in my mind.

Here thou are painted in the dress
Of an inhuman murderess;
Examining upon our hearts
Thy fertile shop of cruel arts:
Engines more keen than ever yet
Adorned a tyrant's cabinet;
Of which the most tormenting are
Black eyes, red lips, and curlèd hair.

But, on the other side, th'art drawn
Like to Aurora in the dawn;
When in the East she slumbering lies,
And stretches out her milky thighs;
While all the morning choir does sing,
And manna falls, and roses spring;
And, at thy feet, the wooing doves
Sit pérfecting their harmless loves.

Like an enchantress here thou show'st,

Vexing thy restless lover's ghost;
And, by a light obscure, dost rave
Over his entrails, in the cave;
Divining thence, with horrid care,
How long thou shalt continue fair;
And (when informed) them throw'st away,
To be the greedy vulture's prey.

But, against that, thou sit'st afloat
Like Venus in her pearly boat.
The halcyons, calming all that's nigh,
Betwixt the air and water fly;
Or, if some rolling wave appears,
A mass of ambergris it bears.
Nor blows more wind than what may well
Convoy the perfume to the smell.

These pictures and a thousand more
Of thee my gallery do store
In all the forms thou canst invent
Either to please me, or torment:
For thou alone to people me,
Art grown a numerous colony;
And a collection choicer far
Than or Whitehall's or Mantua's were.

But, of these pictures and the rest,
That at the entrance likes me best:
Where the same posture, and the look

Remains, with which I first was took:
A tender shepherdess, whose hair
Hangs loosely playing in the air,
Transplanting flowers from the green hill,
To crown her head, and bosom fill.

Young Love

Come, little infant, love me now,
　While thine unsuspected years
Clear thine agèd father's brow
　From cold jealousy and fears.

Pretty, surely, 'twere to see
　By young love old time beguiled,
While our sportings are as free
　As the nurse's with the child.

Common beauties stay fifteen;
　Such as yours should swifter move,
Whose fair blossoms are too green
　Yet for lust, but not for love.

Love as much the snowy lamb,
　Or the wanton kid, does prize,
As the lusty bull or ram,
　For his morning sacrifice.

Now then love me: time may take
　Thee before thy time away:
Of this need we'll virtue make,
　And learn love before we may.

So we win of doubtful fate;
　And if good she to us meant,
We that good shall antedate,

 Or, if ill, that ill prevent.

Thus as kingdoms, frustrating
 Other titles to their crown,
In the cradle crown their king,
 So all foreign claims to drown,

So, to make all rivals vain,
 Now I crown thee with my love:
Crown me with thy love again,
 And we both shall monarchs prove.

The Definition of Love

My love is of a birth as rare
As 'tis for object strange and high;
It was begotten by Despair
Upon Impossibility.

Magnanimous Despair alone
Could show me so divine a thing
Where feeble Hope could ne'er have flown,
But vainly flapp'd its tinsel wing.

And yet I quickly might arrive
Where my extended soul is fixt,
But Fate does iron wedges drive,
And always crowds itself betwixt.

For Fate with jealous eye does see
Two perfect loves, nor lets them close;
Their union would her ruin be,
And her tyrannic pow'r depose.

And therefore her decrees of steel
Us as the distant poles have plac'd,
(Though love's whole world on us doth wheel)
Not by themselves to be embrac'd;

Unless the giddy heaven fall,
And earth some new convulsion tear;
And, us to join, the world should all

Be cramp'd into a planisphere.

As lines, so loves oblique may well
Themselves in every angle greet;
But ours so truly parallel,
Though infinite, can never meet.

Therefore the love which us doth bind,
But Fate so enviously debars,
Is the conjunction of the mind,
And opposition of the stars.

The Fair Singer

To make a final conquest of all me,
Love did compose so sweet an enemy,
In whom both beauties to my death agree,
Joining themselves in fatal harmony;
That while she with her eyes my heart does bind,
She with her voice might captivate my mind.

I could have fled from one but singly fair,
My disentangled soul itself might save,
Breaking the curled trammels of her hair.
But how should I avoid to be her slave,
Whose subtle art invisibly can wreath
My fetters of the very air I breathe?

It had been easy fighting in some plain,
Where victory might hang in equal choice,
But all resistance against her is vain,
Who has th'advantage both of eyes and voice,
And all my forces needs must be undone,
She having gained both the wind and sun.

Damon the Mower

Hark how the Mower Damon sung,
With love of Juliana stung!
While everything did seem to paint
The scene more fit for his complaint.
Like her fair eyes the day was fair,
But scorching like his am'rous care.
Sharp like his scythe his sorrow was,
And withered like his hopes the grass.

'Oh what unusual heats are here,
Which thus our sunburned meadows sear!
The grasshopper its pipe gives o'er;
And hamstringed frogs can dance no more.
But in the brook the green frog wades;
And grasshoppers seek out the shades.
Only the snake, that kept within,
Now glitters in its second skin.

'This heat the sun could never raise,
Nor Dog Star so inflame the days.
It from an higher beauty grow'th,
Which burns the fields and mower both:
Which mads the dog, and makes the sun
Hotter than his own Phaëton.
Not July causeth these extremes,
But Juliana's scorching beams.

'Tell me where I may pass the fires

Of the hot day, or hot desires.
To what cool cave shall I descend,
Or to what gelid fountain bend?
Alas! I look for ease in vain,
When remedies themselves complain.
No moisture but my tears do rest,
Nor cold but in her icy breast.

'How long wilt thou, fair shepherdess,
Esteem me, and my presents less?
To thee the harmless snake I bring,
Disarmèd of its teeth and sting;
To thee chameleons, changing hue,
And oak leaves tipped with honey dew.
Yet thou, ungrateful, hast not sought
Nor what they are, nor who them brought.

'I am the Mower Damon, known
Through all the meadows I have mown.
On me the morn her dew distills
Before her darling daffodils.
And, if at noon my toil me heat,
The sun himself licks off my sweat.
While, going home, the evening sweet
In cowslip-water bathes my feet.

'What, though the piping shepherd stock
The plains with an unnumbered flock,
This scythe of mine discovers wide

More ground than all his sheep do hide.
With this the golden fleece I shear
Of all these closes every year.
And though in wool more poor than they,
Yet am I richer far in hay.

'Nor am I so deformed to sight,
If in my scythe I lookèd right;
In which I see my picture done,
As in a crescent moon the sun.
The deathless fairies take me oft
To lead them in their dances soft:
And, when I tune myself to sing,
About me they contract their ring.

'How happy might I still have mowed,
Had not Love here his thistles sowed!
But now I all the day complain,
Joining my labour to my pain;
And with my scythe cut down the grass,
Yet still my grief is where it was:
But, when the iron blunter grows,
Sighing, I whet my scythe and woes.'

While thus he threw his elbow round,
Depopulating all the ground,
And, with his whistling scythe, does cut
Each stroke between the earth and root,
The edgèd steel by careless chance

Did into his own ankle glance;
And there among the grass fell down,
By his own scythe, the Mower mown.

'Alas!' said he, 'these hurts are slight
To those that die by love's despite.
With shepherd's-purse, and clown's-all-heal,
The blood I staunch, and wound I seal.
Only for him no cure is found,
Whom Juliana's eyes do wound.
'Tis death alone that this must do:
For Death thou art a Mower too.'

The Mower's Song

My mind was once the true survey
    Of all these meadows fresh and gay,
    And in the greenness of the grass
    Did see its hopes as in a glass;
    When Juliana came, and she
What I do to the grass, does to my thoughts and me.

    But these, while I with sorrow pine,
    Grew more luxuriant still and fine,
    That not one blade of grass you spy'd
    But had a flower on either side;
    When Juliana came, and she
What I do to the grass, does to my thoughts and me.

    Unthankful meadows, could you so
    A fellowship so true forgo?
    And in your gaudy May-games meet
    While I lay trodden under feet?
    When Juliana came, and she
What I do to the grass, does to my thoughts and me.

    But what you in compassion ought,
    Shall now by my revenge be wrought;
    And flow'rs, and grass, and I and all,
    Will in one common ruin fall.
    For Juliana comes, and she
What I do to the grass, does to my thoughts and me.

    And thus, ye meadows, which have been
    Companions of my thoughts more green,
    Shall now the heraldry become
    With which I shall adorn my tomb;
    For Juliana comes, and she
What I do to the grass, does to my thoughts and me.

The Mower to the Glow-Worms

Ye living lamps, by whose dear light
The nightingale does sit so late,
And studying all the summer night,
Her matchless songs does meditate;

Ye country comets, that portend
No war nor prince's funeral,
Shining unto no higher end
Than to presage the grass's fall;

Ye glow-worms, whose officious flame
To wand'ring mowers shows the way,
That in the night have lost their aim,
And after foolish fires do stray;

Your courteous lights in vain you waste,
Since Juliana here is come,
For she my mind hath so displac'd
That I shall never find my home.

RICHARD LOVELACE

Song to Amarantha, that she would Dishevel her Hair

    Amarantha sweet and fair
Ah braid no more that shining hair!
    As my curious hand or eye
Hovering round thee let it fly.

    Let it fly as unconfin'd
As its calm ravisher, the wind,
    Who hath left his darling th'East,
To wanton o'er that spicy nest.

    Ev'ry tress must be confest
But neatly tangled at the best;
    Like a clue of golden thread,
Most excellently ravelled.

    Do not then wind up that light
In ribands, and o'er-cloud in night;
    Like the sun in's early ray,
But shake your head and scatter day.

    See 'tis broke! Within this grove
The bower, and the walks of love,
    Weary lie we down and rest,
And fan each other's panting breast.

    Here we'll strip and cool our fire

In cream below, in milk-baths higher:
    And when all wells are drawn dry,
I'll drink a tear out of thine eye,

    Which our very joys shall leave
That sorrows thus we can deceive;
    Or our very sorrows weep,
That joys so ripe, so little keep.

To Althea, from Prison

When Love with unconfinèd wings
    Hovers within my Gates,
And my divine *Althea* brings
    To whisper at the Grates;
When I lie tangled in her hair,
    And fettered to her eye,
The Gods that wanton in the Air,
    Know no such Liberty.

When flowing Cups run swiftly round
    With no allaying *Thames*,
Our careless heads with Roses bound,
    Our hearts with Loyal Flames;
When thirsty grief in Wine we steep,
    When Healths and draughts go free,
Fishes that tipple in the Deep
    Know no such Liberty.

When (like committed linnets) I
    With shriller throat shall sing
The sweetness, Mercy, Majesty,
    And glories of my King;
When I shall voice aloud how good
    He is, how Great should be,
Enlargèd Winds, that curl the Flood,
    Know no such Liberty.

Stone Walls do not a Prison make,

Nor Iron bars a Cage;
Minds innocent and quiet take
   That for an Hermitage.
If I have freedom in my Love,
   And in my soul am free,
Angels alone that soar above,
   Enjoy such Liberty.

The Scrutinie

I

Why should you sweare I am forsworn,
   Since thine I vow'd to be?
Lady it is already Morn,
   And 'twas last night I swore to thee
That fond impossibility.

II

Have I not lov'd thee much and long,
   A tedious twelve houres space?
I must all other Beauties wrong,
   And rob thee of a new imbrace;
Could I still dote upon thy Face.

III

Not, but all joy in thy browne haire,
   By others may be found;
But I must search the blank and faire
   Like skilfull Minerallist's that sound
For Treasure in un-plow'd-up ground.

IV

Then, if when I have lov'd my round,
   Thou prov'st the pleasant she;

With spoyles of meaner Beauties crown'd,
   I laden will returne to thee,
Ev'd sated with Varietie.

To Lucasta, Going to the Wars

Tell me not (Sweet) I am unkind,
        That from the nunnery
Of thy chaste breast and quiet mind
        To war and arms I fly.

True, a new mistress now I chase,
        The first foe in the field;
And with a stronger faith embrace
        A sword, a horse, a shield.

Yet this inconstancy is such
        As you too shall adore;
I could not love thee (Dear) so much,
        Lov'd I not Honour more.

SIR JOHN SUCKLING

Song: Out upon it, I have lov'd

Out upon it, I have lov'd
    Three whole days together;
And am like to love three more,
    If it prove fair weather.

Time shall moult away his wings,
    Ere he shall discover
In the whole wide world again
    Such a constant lover.

But the spite on't is, no praise
    Is due at all to me;
Love with me had made no stays,
    Had it any been but she.

Had it any been but she,
    And that very face,
There had been at least ere this
    A dozen dozen in her place.

Song: Why so pale and wan fond lover?

Why so pale and wan fond lover?
    Prithee why so pale?
Will, when looking well can't move her,
    Looking ill prevail?
    Prithee why so pale?

Why so dull and mute young sinner?
    Prithee why so mute?
Will, when speaking well can't win her,
    Saying nothing do't?
    Prithee why so mute?

Quit, quit for shame, this will not move,
    This cannot take her;
If of herself she will not love,
    Nothing can make her;
    The devil take her.

JOHN WILMOT, EARL OF ROCHESTER

A Song of a Young Lady to Her Ancient Lover

Ancient person, for whom I
All the flattering youth defy,
Long be it ere thou grow old,
Aching, shaking, crazy, cold;
   But still continue as thou art,
   Ancient person of my heart.

On thy withered lips and dry,
Which like barren furrows lie,
Brooding kisses I will pour
Shall thy youthful [heat] restore
(Such kind showers in autumn fall,
And a second spring recall);
   Nor from thee will ever part,
   Ancient person of my heart.

Thy nobler part, which but to name
In our sex would be counted shame,
By age's frozen grasp possessed,
From [his] ice shall be released,
And soothed by my reviving hand,
In former warmth and vigor stand.
All a lover's wish can reach
For thy joy my love shall teach,
And for they pleasure shall improve
All that art can add to love.
   Yet still I love thee without art,

Ancient person of my heart.

A Song: 'Absent from thee I languish still'

ABSENT from thee I languish still,
  Then ask me not, When I return?
The straying fool 'twill plainly kill
  To wish all day, all night to mourn.

Dear, from thine arms then let me fly,
  That my fantastic mind may prove
The torments it deserves to try,
  That tears my fix'd heart from my love.

When, wearied with a world of woe,
  To thy safe bosom I retire,
Where love, and peace, and truth does flow,
  May I, contented, there expire.

Lest once more wandering from that heaven,
  I fall on some base heart unblest,
Faithless to thee, false, unforgiven,
  And lose my everlasting rest.

To His Mistress

Why dost thou shade thy lovely face? O why
Does that eclipsing hand of thine deny
The sunshine of the Sun's enlivening eye?

Without thy light what light remains in me?
Thou art my life; my way, my light's in thee;
I live, I move, and by thy beams I see.

Thou art my life-if thou but turn away
My life's a thousand deaths. Thou art my way-
Without thee, Love, I travel not but stray.

My light thou art-without thy glorious sight
My eyes are darken'd with eternal night.
My Love, thou art my way, my life, my light.

Thou art my way; I wander if thou fly.
Thou art my light; if hid, how blind am I!
Thou art my life; if thou withdraw'st, I die.

My eyes are dark and blind, I cannot see:
To whom or whither should my darkness flee,
But to that light?-and who's that light but thee?

If I have lost my path, dear lover, say,
Shall I still wander in a doubtful way?
Love, shall a lamb of Israel's sheepfold stray?

My path is lost, my wandering steps do stray;
I cannot go, nor can I safely stay;
Whom should I seek but thee, my path, my way?

And yet thou turn'st thy face away and fly'st me!
And yet I sue for grace and thou deny'st me!
Speak, art thou angry, Love, or only try'st me?

Thou art the pilgrim's path, the blind man's eye,
The dead man's life. On thee my hopes rely:
If I but them remove, I surely die.

Dissolve thy sunbeams, close thy wings and stay!
See, see how I am blind, and dead, and stray!
-O thou art my life, my light, my way!

Then work thy will! If passion bid me flee,
My reason shall obey, my wings shall be
Stretch'd out no farther than from me to thee!

APHRA BEHN
Oh, How the Hand the Lover Ought to Prize

Oh, how the hand the lover ought to prize
    'Bove any one peculiar grace!
While he is dying for the eyes
    And doting on the lovely face,
The unconsid'ring little knows
How much he to this beauty owes.

That, when the lover absent is,
    Informs him of his mistress' heart;
'Tis that which gives him all his bliss
    When dear love-secrets 'twill impart:
That plights the faith the maid bestows,
And that confirms the tim'rous vows.

'Tis that betrays the tenderness
    Which the too bashful tongue denies;
'Tis that which does the heart confess,
    And spares the language of the eyes;
'Tis that which treasure gives so vast,
Ev'n Iris 'twill to Damon give at last.

Love Armed

Song from Abdelazar

Love in Fantastic Triumph sat,
Whilst Bleeding Hearts around him flowed,
For whom Fresh pains he did Create,
And strange Tyrannic power he showed;
From thy Bright Eyes he took his fire,
Which round about, in sport he hurled;
But 'twas from mine he took desire
Enough to undo the Amorous World.

From me he took his sighs and tears,
From thee his Pride and Cruelty;
From me his Languishments and Fears,
And every Killing Dart from thee;
Thus thou and I, the God have armed,
And set him up a Deity;
But my poor Heart alone is harmed,
Whilst thine the Victor is, and free.

Love's Witness

Slight unpremeditated Words are borne
    By every common Wind into the Air;
Carelessly utter'd, die as soon as born,
    And in one instant give both Hope and Fear:
Breathing all Contraries with the same Wind
According to the Caprice of the Mind.

But *Billetdoux* are constant Witnesses,
    Substantial Records to Eternity;
Just Evidences, who the Truth confess,
    On which the Lover safely may rely;
They're serious Thoughts, digested and resolv'd;
And last, when Words are into Clouds devolv'd.

The Willing Mistriss

Amyntas led me to a Grove,
    Where all the Trees did shade us;
The Sun it self, though it had Strove,
    It could not have betray'd us:
The place secur'd from humane Eyes,
    No other fear allows.
But when the Winds that gently rise,
    Doe Kiss the yielding Boughs.

Down there we satt upon the Moss,
    And id begin to play
A Thousand Amorous Tricks, to pass
    The heat of all the day.
A many Kisses he did give:
    And I return'd the same
Which made me willing to receive
    That which I dare not name.

His Charming Eyes no Aid requir'd
    To tell their softning Tale;
On her that was already fir'd
    'Twas easy to prevaile.
He did but Kiss and Clasp me round,
    Whilst those his thoughts Exprest:
And lay'd me gently on the Ground;
    Ah who can guess the rest?

WILLIAM BLAKE

Never Seek to Tell thy Love

Never seek to tell thy love
Love that never told can be
For the gentle wind does move
Silently invisibly

I told my love I told my love
I told her all my heart
Trembling cold in ghastly fears
Ah she doth depart

Soon as she was gone from me
A traveller came by
Silently invisibly
O was no deny

The Sick Rose

O Rose thou art sick.
The invisible worm,
That flies in the night
In the howling storm:

Has found out thy bed
Of crimson joy:
And his dark secret love
Does thy life destroy.

The Clod and the Pebble

"Love seeketh not itself to please,
Nor for itself hath any care,
But for another gives its ease,
And builds a Heaven in Hell's despair."

So sung a little Clod of Clay
Trodden with the cattle's feet,
But a Pebble of the brook
Warbled out these metres meet:

"Love seeketh only self to please,
To bind another to its delight,
Joys in another's loss of ease,
And builds a Hell in Heaven's despite."

The Garden of Love

I went to the Garden of Love,
And saw what I never had seen:
A Chapel was built in the midst,
Where I used to play on the green.

And the gates of this Chapel were shut,
And Thou shalt not. writ over the door;
So I turn'd to the Garden of Love,
That so many sweet flowers bore.

And I saw it was filled with graves,
And tomb-stones where flowers should be:
And Priests in black gowns, were walking their rounds,
And binding with briars, my joys & desires.

ROBERT BURNS
A Red, Red Rose

O my Luve's like a red, red rose,
    That's newly sprung in June;
O my Luve's like the melodie
    That's sweetly play'd in tune.

As fair are thou, my bonie lass,
    So deep in luve am I;
And I will luve thee still, my Dear,
    Till a' the seas gang dry.

Till a' the seas gang dry, my Dear,
    And the rocks melt wi' the sun:
I will luve thee still, my dear,
    While the sands o' life shall run.

And fare thee weel, my only Luve!
    And fare thee weel, a while!
And I will come again, my Luve,
    Tho' it were ten thousand mile!

Ae Fond Kiss

Ae fond kiss, and then we sever;
Ae fareweel, and then forever!
Deep in heart-wrung tears   I'll pledge thee,
Warring sighs and groans I'll wage thee.
Who shall say that Fortune grieves him,
While the star of hope she leaves him?
Me, nae cheerfu' twinkle lights me;
Dark despair around benights me.

I'll ne'er blame my partial fancy,
Naething could resist my Nancy;
But to see her was to love her;
Love but her, and love forever.
Had we never lov'd sae kindly,
Had we never lov'd sae blindly,
Never met—or never parted—
We had ne'er been broken-hearted.

Fare thee weel, thou first and fairest!
Fare thee weel, thou best and dearest!
Thine be ilka joy and treasure,
Peace. enjoyment, love, and pleasure!
Ae fond kiss, and then we sever;
Ae fareweel, alas, forever!
Deep in heart-wrung tears   I'll pledge thee,
Warring sighs and groans I'll wage thee!

WILLIAM WORDSWORTH

She Dwelt among the Untrodden Ways

She dwelt among the untrodden ways
    Beside the springs of Dove,
A Maid whom there were none to praise
    And very few to love:

A violet by a mossy stone
    Half hidden from the eye!
—Fair as a star, when only one
    Is shining in the sky.

She lived unknown, and few could know
    When Lucy ceased to be;
But she is in her grave, and, oh,
    The difference to me!

She Was a Phantom of Delight

She was a Phantom of delight
When first she gleamed upon my sight;
A lovely Apparition, sent
To be a moment's ornament;
Her eyes as stars of Twilight fair;
Like Twilight's, too, her dusky hair;
But all things else about her drawn
From May-time and the cheerful Dawn;
A dancing Shape, an Image gay,
To haunt, to startle, and way-lay.
I saw her upon nearer view,
A Spirit, yet a Woman too!
Her household motions light and free,
And steps of virgin-liberty;
A countenance in which did meet
Sweet records, promises as sweet;
A Creature not too bright or good
For human nature's daily food;
For transient sorrows, simple wiles,
Praise, blame, love, kisses, tears, and smiles.
And now I see with eye serene
The very pulse of the machine;
A Being breathing thoughtful breath,
A Traveller between life and death;
The reason firm, the temperate will,
Endurance, foresight, strength, and skill;
A perfect Woman, nobly planned,
To warn, to comfort, and command;

And yet a Spirit still, and bright
With something of angelic light.

"Why art thou silent! Is thy love a plant"

Why art thou silent! Is thy love a plant
Of such weak fibre that the treacherous air
Of absence withers what was once so fair?
Is there no debt to pay, no boon to grant?
Yet have my thoughts for thee been vigilant—
Bound to thy service with unceasing care,
The mind's least generous wish a mendicant
For nought but what thy happiness could spare.
Speak— though this soft warm heart, once free to hold
A thousand tender pleasures, thine and mine,
Be left more desolate, more dreary cold
Than a forsaken bird's-nest filled with snow
'Mid its own bush of leafless eglantine—
Speak, that my torturing doubts their end may know.

LORD BYRON

She Walks in Beauty

She walks in beauty, like the night
   Of cloudless climes and starry skies;
And all that's best of dark and bright
   Meet in her aspect and her eyes;
Thus mellowed to that tender light
   Which heaven to gaudy day denies.

One shade the more, one ray the less,
   Had half impaired the nameless grace
Which waves in every raven tress,
   Or softly lightens o'er her face;
Where thoughts serenely sweet express,
   How pure, how dear their dwelling-place.

And on that cheek, and o'er that brow,
   So soft, so calm, yet eloquent,
The smiles that win, the tints that glow,
   But tell of days in goodness spent,
A mind at peace with all below,
   A heart whose love is innocent!

WHEN we two parted
In silence and tears,
Half broken-hearted
To sever for years,
Pale grew thy cheek and cold,
Colder thy kiss;
Truly that hour foretold
Sorrow to this.

The dew of the morning
Sunk chill on my brow--
It felt like the warning
Of what I feel now.
Thy vows are all broken,
And light is thy fame:
I hear thy name spoken,
And share in its shame.

They name thee before me,
A knell to mine ear;
A shudder comes o'er me--
Why wert thou so dear?
They know not I knew thee,
Who knew thee too well:
Lond, long shall I rue thee,
Too deeply to tell.

I secret we met--
I silence I grieve,
That thy heart could forget,
Thy spirit deceive.
If I should meet thee
After long years,
How should I greet thee?
With silence and tears.

PERCY BYSSHE SHELLEY
To Jane: The Invitation

Best and brightest, come away!
Fairer far than this fair Day,
Which, like thee to those in sorrow,
Comes to bid a sweet good-morrow
To the rough Year just awake
In its cradle on the brake.
The Brightest hour of unborn Spring,
Through the winter wandering,
Found, it seems, the halcyon Morn
To hoar February born.
Bending from Heaven, in azure mirth,
It kissed the forehead of the Earth,
And smiled upon the silent sea,
And bade the frozen streams be free,
And waked to music all their fountains,
And breathed upon the frozen mountains,
And like a prophetess of May
Strewed flowers upon the barren way,
Making the wintry world appear
Like one on whom thou smilest, dear.
Away, away, from men and towns,
To the wild wood and the downs—
To the silent wilderness
Where the soul need not repress
Its music lest it should not find
An echo in another's mind.
While the touch of Nature's art

Harmonizes heart to heart.
I leave this notice on my door
For each accustomed visitor:—
"I am gone into the fields
To take what this sweet hour yields;—
Reflection, you may come tomorrow,
Sit by the fireside with Sorrow.—
You with the unpaid bill, Despair,—
You, tiresome verse-reciter, Care,—
I will pay you in the grave,—
Death will listen to your stave.
Expectation too, be off!
Today is for itself enough;
Hope, in pity mock not Woe
With smiles, nor follow where I go;
Long having lived on thy sweet food,
At length I find one moment's good
After long pain—with all your love,
This you never told me of."

Radiant Sister of the Day,
Awake! arise! And come away!
To the wild woods and the plains,
And the pools where winter rains
Image all their roof of leaves,
Where the pine its garland weaves
Of sapless green, and ivy dun
Round stems that never kiss the sun:
Where the lawns and pastures be,

And the sandhills of the sea:—
Where the melting hoar-frost wets
The daisy-star that never sets,
And wind-flowers, and violets,
Which yet join not scent to hue,
Crown the pale year weak and new;
When the night is left behind
In the deep east, dun and blind,
And the blue noon is over us,
And the multitudinous
Billows murmur at our feet,
Where the earth and ocean meet,
And all things seem only one
In the universal sun.

The Indian Serenade

I arise from dreams of thee
In the first sweet sleep of night,
When the winds are breathing low,
And the stars are shining bright:
I arise from dreams of thee,
And a spirit in my feet
Hath led me—who knows how?
To thy chamber window, Sweet!

The wandering airs they faint
On the dark, the silent stream—
The Champak odours fail
Like sweet thoughts in a dream;
The Nightingale's complaint,
It dies upon her heart;—
As I must on thine,
Oh, belovèd as thou art!

Oh lift me from the grass!
I die! I faint! I fail!
Let thy love in kisses rain
On my lips and eyelids pale.
My cheek is cold and white, alas!
My heart beats loud and fast;—
Oh! press it to thine own again,
Where it will break at last.

Love's Philosophy

The fountains mingle with the river
   And the rivers with the ocean,
The winds of heaven mix for ever
   With a sweet emotion;
Nothing in the world is single;
   All things by a law divine
In one spirit meet and mingle.
   Why not I with thine?—

See the mountains kiss high heaven
   And the waves clasp one another;
No sister-flower would be forgiven
   If it disdained its brother;
And the sunlight clasps the earth
   And the moonbeams kiss the sea:
What is all this sweet work worth
   If thou kiss not me?

JOHN KEATS

"Bright star, would I were stedfast as thou art"

Bright star, would I were stedfast as thou art—
    Not in lone splendour hung aloft the night
And watching, with eternal lids apart,
    Like nature's patient, sleepless Eremite,
The moving waters at their priestlike task
    Of pure ablution round earth's human shores,
Or gazing on the new soft-fallen mask
    Of snow upon the mountains and the moors—
No—yet still stedfast, still unchangeable,
    Pillow'd upon my fair love's ripening breast,
To feel for ever its soft fall and swell,
    Awake for ever in a sweet unrest,
Still, still to hear her tender-taken breath,
And so live ever—or else swoon to death.

"This living hand, now warm and capable"

This living hand, now warm and capable
Of earnest grasping, would, if it were cold
And in the icy silence of the tomb,
So haunt thy days and chill thy dreaming nights
That thou would wish thine own heart dry of blood
So in my veins red life might stream again,
And thou be conscience-calm'd–see here it is–
I hold it towards you.

To Fanny

I cry your mercy—pity—love! Aye, love!
   Merciful love that tantalizes not,
One-thoughted, never-wandering, guileless love,
   Unmasked, and being seen—without a blot!
O! let me have thee whole,—all—all—be mine!
   That shape, that fairness, that sweet minor zest
Of love, your kiss,—those hands, those eyes divine,
   That warm, white, lucent, million-pleasured breast,—
Yourself—your soul—in pity give me all,
   Withhold no atom's atom or I die,
Or living on perhaps, your wretched thrall,
   Forget, in the mist of idle misery,
Life's purposes,—the palate of my mind
   Losing its gust, and my ambition blind!

La Belle Dame sans Merci: A Ballad

O what can ail thee, knight-at-arms,
    Alone and palely loitering?
The sedge has withered from the lake,
    And no birds sing.

O what can ail thee, knight-at-arms,
    So haggard and so woe-begone?
The squirrel's granary is full,
    And the harvest's done.

I see a lily on thy brow,
    With anguish moist and fever-dew,
And on thy cheeks a fading rose
    Fast withereth too.

I met a lady in the meads,
    Full beautiful—a faery's child,
Her hair was long, her foot was light,
    And her eyes were wild.

I made a garland for her head,
    And bracelets too, and fragrant zone;
She looked at me as she did love,
    And made sweet moan

I set her on my pacing steed,
    And nothing else saw all day long,
For sidelong would she bend, and sing

A faery's song.

She found me roots of relish sweet,
    And honey wild, and manna-dew,
And sure in language strange she said—
    'I love thee true'.

She took me to her Elfin grot,
    And there she wept and sighed full sore,
And there I shut her wild wild eyes
    With kisses four.

And there she lullèd me asleep,
    And there I dreamed—Ah! woe betide!—
The latest dream I ever dreamt
    On the cold hill side.

I saw pale kings and princes too,
    Pale warriors, death-pale were they all;
They cried—'La Belle Dame sans Merci
    Thee hath in thrall!'

I saw their starved lips in the gloam,
    With horrid warning gapèd wide,
And I awoke and found me here,
    On the cold hill's side.

And this is why I sojourn here,
    Alone and palely loitering,

Though the sedge is withered from the lake,
    And no birds sing.

EMILY BRONTË

Remembrance

Cold in the earth—and the deep snow piled above thee,
Far, far removed, cold in the dreary grave!
Have I forgot, my only Love, to love thee,
Severed at last by Time's all-severing wave?

Now, when alone, do my thoughts no longer hover
Over the mountains, on that northern shore,
Resting their wings where heath and fern-leaves cover
Thy noble heart forever, ever more?

Cold in the earth—and fifteen wild Decembers,
From those brown hills, have melted into spring:
Faithful, indeed, is the spirit that remembers
After such years of change and suffering!

Sweet Love of youth, forgive, if I forget thee,
While the world's tide is bearing me along;
Other desires and other hopes beset me,
Hopes which obscure, but cannot do thee wrong!

No later light has lightened up my heaven,
No second morn has ever shone for me;
All my life's bliss from thy dear life was given,
All my life's bliss is in the grave with thee.

But, when the days of golden dreams had perished,
And even Despair was powerless to destroy,

Then did I learn how existence could be cherished,
Strengthened, and fed without the aid of joy.

Then did I check the tears of useless passion—
Weaned my young soul from yearning after thine;
Sternly denied its burning wish to hasten
Down to that tomb already more than mine.

And, even yet, I dare not let it languish,
Dare not indulge in memory's rapturous pain;
Once drinking deep of that divinest anguish,
How could I seek the empty world again?

Love and Friendship

Love is like the wild rose-briar,
Friendship like the holly-tree—
The holly is dark when the rose-briar blooms
But which will bloom most constantly?

The wild rose-briar is sweet in spring,
Its summer blossoms scent the air;
Yet wait till winter comes again
And who will call the wild-briar fair?

Then scorn the silly rose-wreath now
And deck thee with the holly's sheen,
That when December blights thy brow
He still may leave thy garland green.

ELIZABETH BARRETT BROWNING

Sonnets from the Portuguese 14: If thou must love me, let it be for nought

If thou must love me, let it be for nought
Except for love's sake only. Do not say
I love her for her smile ... her look ... her way
Of speaking gently, ... for a trick of thought
That falls in well with mine, and certes brought
A sense of pleasant ease on such a day'—
For these things in themselves, Belovèd, may
Be changed, or change for thee,—and love, so wrought,
May be unwrought so. Neither love me for
Thine own dear pity's wiping my cheeks dry,—
A creature might forget to weep, who bore
Thy comfort long, and lose thy love thereby!
But love me for love's sake, that evermore
Thou may'st love on, through love's eternity.

Sonnets from the Portuguese 28: My letters! all dead paper, ... mute and white!

My letters! all dead paper, ... mute and white ! —
And yet they seem alive and quivering
Against my tremulous hands which loose the string
And let them drop down on my knee to-night.
This said, ... he wished to have me in his sight
Once, as a friend: this fixed a day in spring
To come and touch my hand ... a simple thing,
Yet I wept for it! — this, ... the paper's light ...
Said, *Dear, I love thee*; and I sank and quailed
As if God's future thundered on my past.
This said, *I am thine* — and so its ink has paled
With lying at my heart that beat too fast.
And this ... O Love, thy words have ill availed,
If, what this said, I dared repeat at last!

Sonnets from the Portuguese 38: First time he kissed me, he but only kissed

First time he kissed me, he but only kissed

The fingers of this hand wherewith I write,

And ever since it grew more clean and white,...

Slow to world-greetings...quick with its "Oh, list,"

When the angels speak. A ring of amethyst

I could not wear here plainer to my sight,

Than that first kiss. The second passed in height

The first, and sought the forehead, and half missed,

Half falling on the hair. O beyond meed!

That was the chrism of love, which love's own crown,

With sanctifying sweetness, did precede.

The third, upon my lips, was folded down

In perfect, purple state! since when, indeed,

I have been proud and said, "My Love, my own."

Sonnets from the Portuguese 43: How do I love thee? Let me count the ways

How do I love thee? Let me count the ways.
I love thee to the depth and breadth and height
My soul can reach, when feeling out of sight
For the ends of being and ideal grace.
I love thee to the level of every day's
Most quiet need, by sun and candle-light.
I love thee freely, as men strive for right;
I love thee purely, as they turn from praise.
I love thee with the passion put to use
In my old griefs, and with my childhood's faith.
I love thee with a love I seemed to lose
With my lost saints. I love thee with the breath,
Smiles, tears, of all my life; and, if God choose,
I shall but love thee better after death.

Sonnets from the Portuguese 44: Beloved, thou has brought me many flowers

Beloved, thou hast brought me many flowers
    Plucked in the garden, all the summer through
    And winter, and it seemed as if they grew
In this close room, nor missed the sun and showers,
So, in the like name of that love of ours,
    Take back these thoughts which here unfolded too,
    And which on warm and cold days I withdrew
From my heart's ground. Indeed, those beds and bowers
    Be overgrown with bitter weeds and rue,
And wait thy weeding; yet here's eglantine,
    Here's ivy!— take them, as I used to do
Thy flowers, and keep them where they shall not pine.
    Instruct thine eyes to keep their colours true,
And tell thy soul, their roots are left in mine.

CHRISTINA ROSSETTI
"I loved you first: but afterwards your love"

I loved you first: but afterwards your love
    Outsoaring mine, sang such a loftier song
As drowned the friendly cooings of my dove.
    Which owes the other most? my love was long,
    And yours one moment seemed to wax more strong;
I loved and guessed at you, you construed me
And loved me for what might or might not be –
    Nay, weights and measures do us both a wrong.
For verily love knows not 'mine' or 'thine;'
    With separate 'I' and 'thou' free love has done,
        For one is both and both are one in love:
Rich love knows nought of 'thine that is not mine;'
        Both have the strength and both the length thereof,
Both of us, of the love which makes us one.

"I wish I could remember that first day"

    I wish I could remember that first day,
        First hour, first moment of your meeting me,
        If bright or dim the season, it might be
Summer or Winter for aught I can say;
So unrecorded did it slip away,
        So blind was I to see and to foresee,
        So dull to mark the budding of my tree
That would not blossom yet for many a May.
If only I could recollect it, such
        A day of days! I let it come and go
        As traceless as a thaw of bygone snow;
It seemed to mean so little, meant so much;
If only now I could recall that touch,
        First touch of hand in hand – Did one but know!

Remember

Remember me when I am gone away,
      Gone far away into the silent land;
      When you can no more hold me by the hand,
Nor I half turn to go yet turning stay.
Remember me when no more day by day
      You tell me of our future that you plann'd:
      Only remember me; you understand
It will be late to counsel then or pray.
Yet if you should forget me for a while
      And afterwards remember, do not grieve:
      For if the darkness and corruption leave
      A vestige of the thoughts that once I had,
Better by far you should forget and smile
      Than that you should remember and be sad.

When I am dead, my dearest

When I am dead, my dearest,
    Sing no sad songs for me;
Plant thou no roses at my head,
    Nor shady cypress tree:
Be the green grass above me
    With showers and dewdrops wet;
And if thou wilt, remember,
    And if thou wilt, forget.

I shall not see the shadows,
    I shall not feel the rain;
I shall not hear the nightingale
    Sing on, as if in pain:
And dreaming through the twilight
    That doth not rise nor set,
Haply I may remember,
    And haply may forget.

Echo

Come to me in the silence of the night;
   Come in the speaking silence of a dream;
Come with soft rounded cheeks and eyes as bright
    As sunlight on a stream;
      Come back in tears,
O memory, hope, love of finished years.

Oh dream how sweet, too sweet, too bitter sweet,
   Whose wakening should have been in Paradise,
Where souls brimfull of love abide and meet;
    Where thirsting longing eyes
      Watch the slow door
That opening, letting in, lets out no more.

Yet come to me in dreams, that I may live
   My very life again tho' cold in death:
Come back to me in dreams, that I may give
    Pulse for pulse, breath for breath:
      Speak low, lean low,
As long ago, my love, how long ago.

THOMAS HARDY
Neutral Tones

We stood by a pond that winter day,
And the sun was white, as though chidden of God,
And a few leaves lay on the starving sod;
    – They had fallen from an ash, and were gray.

Your eyes on me were as eyes that rove
Over tedious riddles of years ago;
And some words played between us to and fro
    On which lost the more by our love.

The smile on your mouth was the deadest thing
Alive enough to have strength to die;
And a grin of bitterness swept thereby
    Like an ominous bird a-wing....

Since then, keen lessons that love deceives,
And wrings with wrong, have shaped to me
Your face, and the God curst sun, and a tree,
    And a pond edged with grayish leaves.

The Voice

Woman much missed, how you call to me, call to me,
Saying that now you are not as you were
When you had changed from the one who was all to me,
But as at first, when our day was fair.

Can it be you that I hear? Let me view you, then,
Standing as when I drew near to the town
Where you would wait for me: yes, as I knew you then,
Even to the original air-blue gown!

Or is it only the breeze, in its listlessness
Travelling across the wet mead to me here,
You being ever dissolved to wan wistlessness,
Heard no more again far or near?

    Thus I; faltering forward,
    Leaves around me falling,
Wind oozing thin through the thorn from norward,
    And the woman calling.

The Phantom Horsewoman

I

Queer are the ways of a man I know:
      He comes and stands
      In a careworn craze,
      And looks at the sands
      And the seaward haze
      With moveless hands
      And face and gaze,
      Then turns to go...
And what does he see when he gazes so?

II

They say he sees as an instant thing
      More clear than to-day,
      A sweet soft scene
      That once was in play
      By that briny green;
      Yes, notes alway
      Warm, real, and keen,
      What his back years bring—
A phantom of his own figuring.

III

Of this vision of his they might say more:
      Not only there

  Does he see this sight,
  But everywhere
  In his brain—day, night,
  As if on the air
  It were drawn rose bright—
  Yea, far from that shore
Does he carry this vision of heretofore:

IV

A ghost-girl-rider. And though, toil-tried,
  He withers daily,
  Time touches her not,
  But she still rides gaily
  In his rapt thought
  On that shagged and shaly
  Atlantic spot,
  And as when first eyed
Draws rein and sings to the swing of the tide.

The Ruined Maid

"O 'Melia, my dear, this does everything crown!
Who could have supposed I should meet you in Town?
And whence such fair garments, such prosperi-ty?" —
"O didn't you know I'd been ruined?" said she.

— "You left us in tatters, without shoes or socks,
Tired of digging potatoes, and spudding up docks;
And now you've gay bracelets and bright feathers three!" —
"Yes: that's how we dress when we're ruined," said she.

— "At home in the barton you said 'thee' and 'thou,'
And 'thik oon,' and 'theäs oon,' and 't'other'; but now
Your talking quite fits 'ee for high compa-ny!" —
"Some polish is gained with one's ruin," said she.

— "Your hands were like paws then, your face blue and bleak
But now I'm bewitched by your delicate cheek,
And your little gloves fit as on any la-dy!" —
"We never do work when we're ruined," said she.

— "You used to call home-life a hag-ridden dream,
And you'd sigh, and you'd sock; but at present you seem
To know not of megrims or melancho-ly!" —
"True. One's pretty lively when ruined," said she.

— "I wish I had feathers, a fine sweeping gown,
And a delicate face, and could strut about Town!" —
"My dear — a raw country girl, such as you be,

Cannot quite expect that. You ain't ruined," said she.

ERNEST DOWSON

Non sum qualis eram bonae sub regno Cynarae

Last night, ah, yesternight, betwixt her lips and mine
There fell thy shadow, Cynara! thy breath was shed
Upon my soul between the kisses and the wine;
And I was desolate and sick of an old passion,
    Yea, I was desolate and bowed my head:
I have been faithful to thee, Cynara! in my fashion.

All night upon mine heart I felt her warm heart beat,
Night-long within mine arms in love and sleep she lay;
Surely the kisses of her bought red mouth were sweet;
But I was desolate and sick of an old passion,
    When I awoke and found the dawn was grey:
I have been faithful to thee, Cynara! in my fashion.

I have forgot much, Cynara! gone with the wind,
Flung roses, roses riotously with the throng,
Dancing, to put thy pale, lost lilies out of mind,
But I was desolate and sick of an old passion,
    Yea, all the time, because the dance was long:
I have been faithful to thee, Cynara! in my fashion.

I cried for madder music and for stronger wine,
But when the feast is finished and the lamps expire,
Then falls thy shadow, Cynara! the night is thine;
And I am desolate and sick of an old passion,

Yea, hungry for the lips of my desire:
I have been faithful to thee, Cynara! in my fashion.

What Is Love?

WHAT is Love?
      Is it a folly,
      Is it mirth, or melancholy?
Joys above,
      Are there many, or not any?
What is Love?
If you please,
A most sweet folly!
      Full of mirth and melancholy:
Both of these!
      In its sadness worth all gladness,
If you please!
Prithee where,
      Goes Love a-hiding?
      Is he long in his abiding
Anywhere?
      Can you bind him when you find him;
Prithee, where?
With spring days
      Love comes and dallies:
      Upon the mountains, through the valleys
Lie Love's ways.
      Then he leaves you and deceives you
In spring days.

CHARLOTTE MEW

The Farmer's Bride

Three summers since I chose a maid,
Too young maybe—but more's to do
At harvest-time than bide and woo.
    When us was wed she turned afraid
Of love and me and all things human;
Like the shut of a winter's day
Her smile went out, and 'twadn't a woman—
    More like a little frightened fay.
        One night, in the Fall, she runned away.

"Out 'mong the sheep, her be," they said,
'Should properly have been abed;
But sure enough she wadn't there
Lying awake with her wide brown stare.
So over seven-acre field and up-along across the down
    We chased her, flying like a hare
    Before out lanterns. To Church-Town
        All in a shiver and a scare
    We caught her, fetched her home at last
        And turned the key upon her, fast.

She does the work about the house
As well as most, but like a mouse:
    Happy enough to chat and play
    With birds and rabbits and such as they,

So long as men-folk keep away.
"Not near, not near!" her eyes beseech
When one of us comes within reach.
  The women say that beasts in stall
  Look round like children at her call.
  I've hardly heard her speak at all.

Shy as a leveret, swift as he,
Straight and slight as a young larch tree,
Sweet as the first wild violets, she,
To her wild self. But what to me?

The short days shorten and the oaks are brown,
  The blue smoke rises to the low grey sky,
One leaf in the still air falls slowly down,
  A magpie's spotted feathers lie
On the black earth spread white with rime,
The berries redden up to Christmas-time.
  What's Christmas-time without there be
  Some other in the house than we!

  She sleeps up in the attic there
  Alone, poor maid. 'Tis but a stair
Betwixt us. Oh! my God! the down,
 The soft young down of her, the brown,
The brown of her—her eyes, her hair, her hair!

Printed in Great Britain
by Amazon